First published in Great Britain in 2009 by

Quercus
21 Bloomsbury Square
London
WC1A 2NS

A CIP catalogue record for this book is available from the British Library

ISBN 978 1 84866 024 3

Printed and bound in China

10 9 8 7 6 5 4 3 2 1

Layout, picture research and authoring by Pikaia Imaging

What's up DOG?

Quercus

NAME: DONALD
AGE: 7
LIVES: PALM BEACH

I've a feeling I've been running around in circles

4

NAME: VERNE
AGE: 9
LIVES: AMARILLO

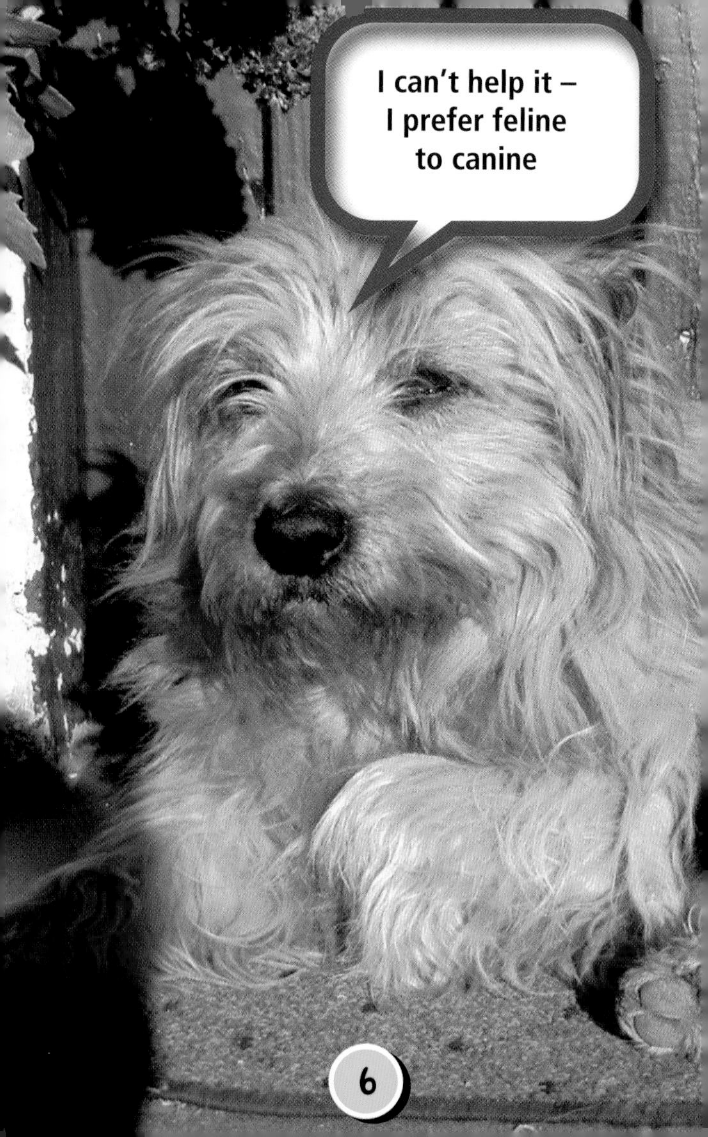
I can't help it – I prefer feline to canine

NAME: FELIX
AGE: 6
LIVES: CONNECTICAT

NAME: LOU-LOU
AGE: 6
LIVES: NEW LONDON

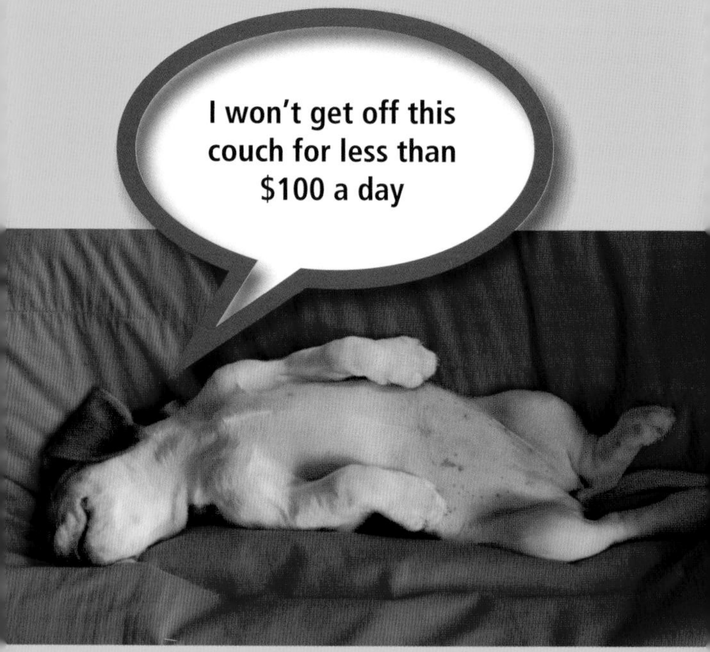

I'm always in the dog house

NAME: BARNEY
AGE: 3
LIVES: HOUSTON

9

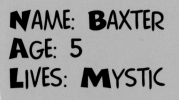

NAME: BAXTER
AGE: 5
LIVES: MYSTIC

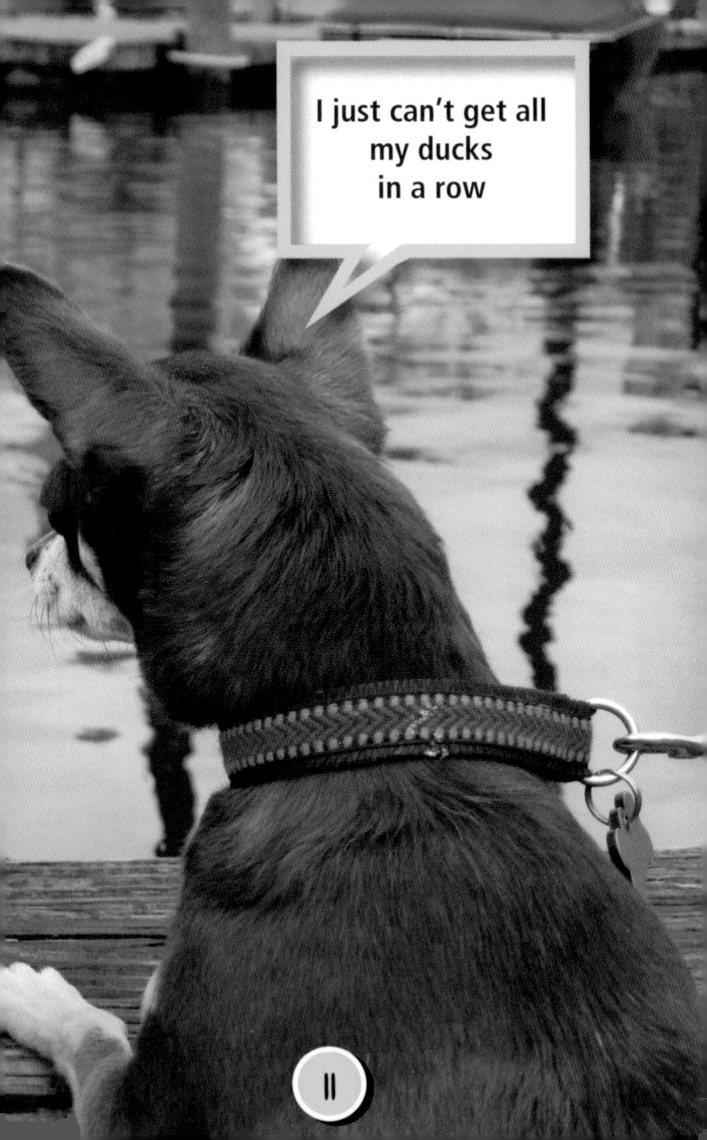
I just can't get all my ducks in a row

NAME: HOTSPUR
AGE: 6
LIVES: LA JOLLA
Sometimes I think I might be out of my depth

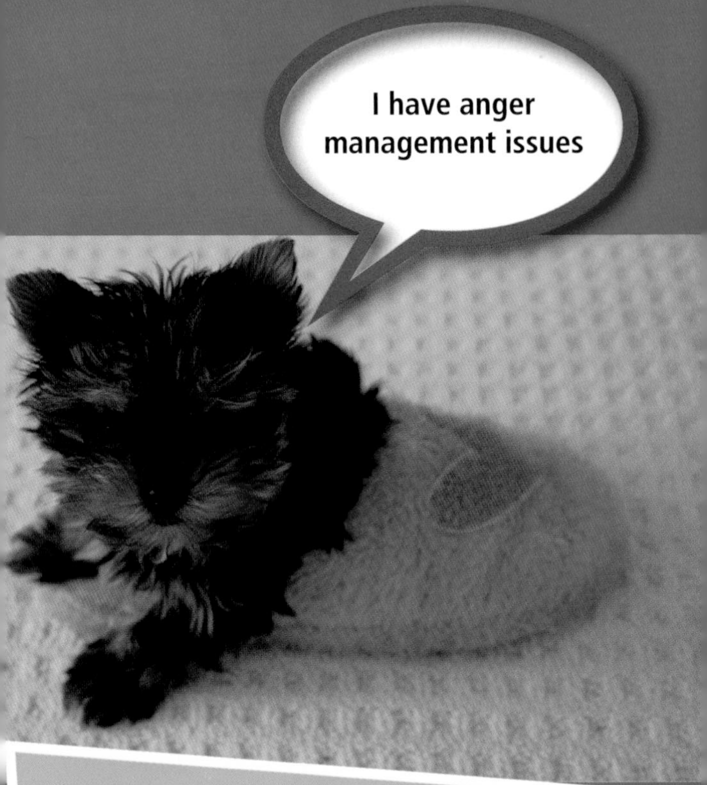

NAME: ANGUS
AGE: 1
LIVES: ATLANTA

NAME: BERNARD
AGE: 8
LIVES: NEW ORLEANS

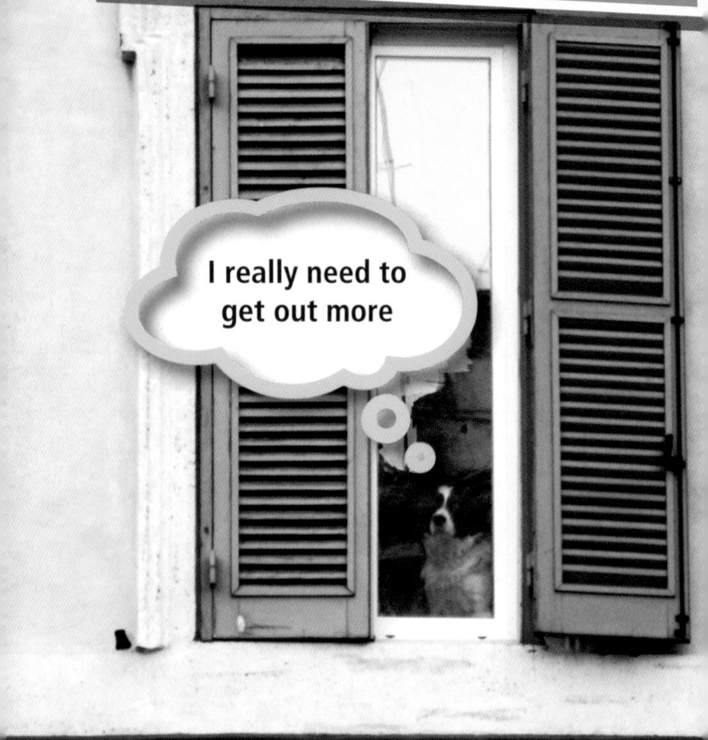

I'm worried that I intimidate people

NAME: TYSON
AGE: 4
LIVES: ORLANDO

Why do mailmen laugh at me?

NAME: LUCIFER
AGE: 7
LIVES: LONG ISLAND

NAME: **WOLFIE**
AGE: 5
LIVES: **PORTLAND**

I find I'm always
barking up the
wrong tree

NAME: BASIL
AGE: 6
LIVES: NORFOLK VA

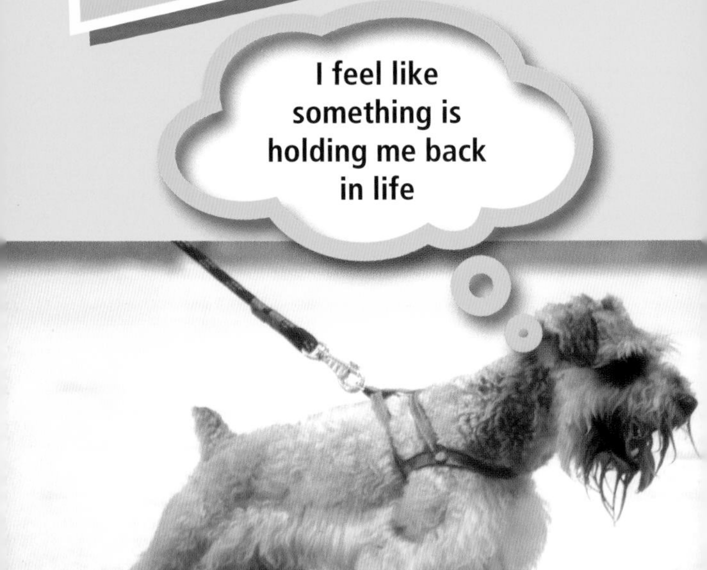

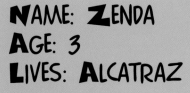

NAME: ZENDA
AGE: 3
LIVES: ALCATRAZ

19

I'm feeling a bit puffed-up at the moment

NAME: GEORGE
AGE: 5
LIVES: ANCHORAGE

Sometimes I don’t
know which way
to turn

NAME: CUSTER
AGE: 3
LIVES: SACRAMENTO

I've had a lot of problems with the landlord

NAME: IVANA
AGE: 7
LIVES: SALT LAKE CITY

NAME: HITCHCOCK
AGE: 6
LIVES: LOUISIANA

I can't stand heights!

Just before the dinner bell I lose the will to live

NAME: SMIFFY
AGE: 3
LIVES: FRESNO

NAME: CARRIE
AGE: 2
LIVES: MANHATTAN

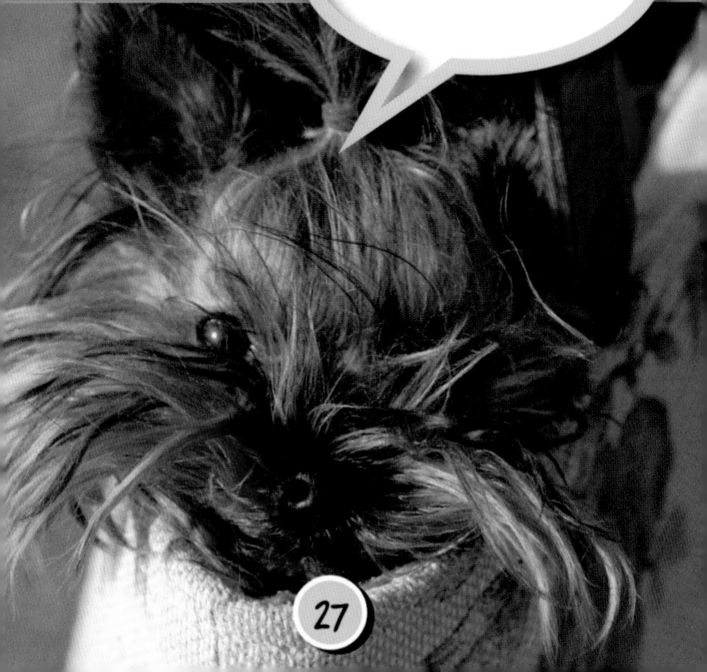

NAME: GOLDIE
AGE: 4
LIVES: PHOENIX

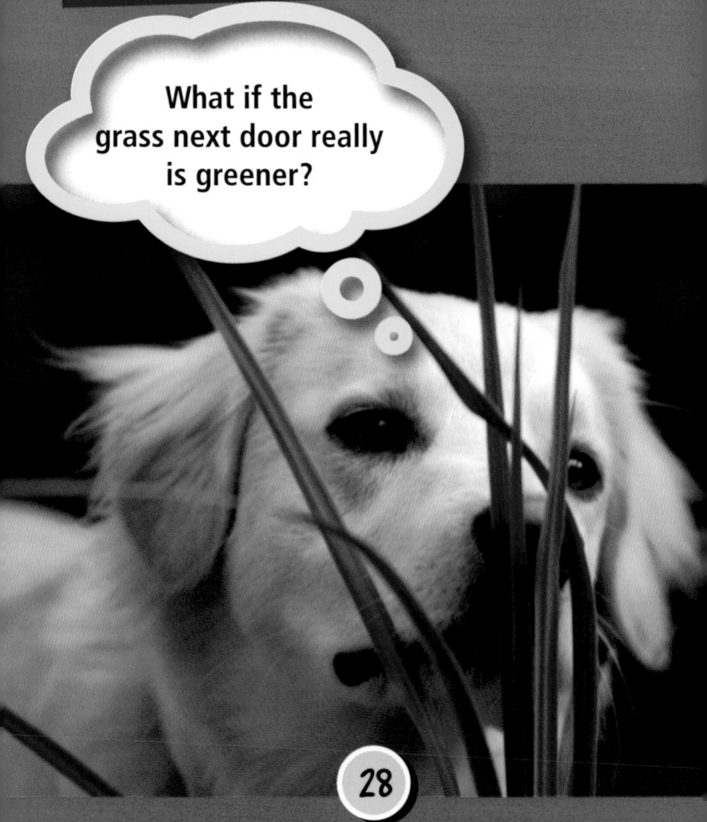

Oh no... there are cats everywhere! If I close my eyes long enough will they all be gone?

NAME: GERALD
AGE: 3
LIVES: TWIN FALLS

NAME: **LEONARDO**
AGE: 7
LIVES: **PORTLAND**

I'm losing my perspective

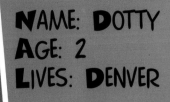

Every day seems to be a dog day

NAME: LEONARD
AGE: 3
LIVES: ST LOUIS

NAME: HERBERT
AGE: 2
LIVES: ANCHORAGE

If I'm a dog, why aren't I hot?

Why do my blind dates all go so badly?

NAME: HERMAN
AGE: 9
LIVES: SALEM

NAME: GLADSTONE
AGE: 3
LIVES: BOSTON

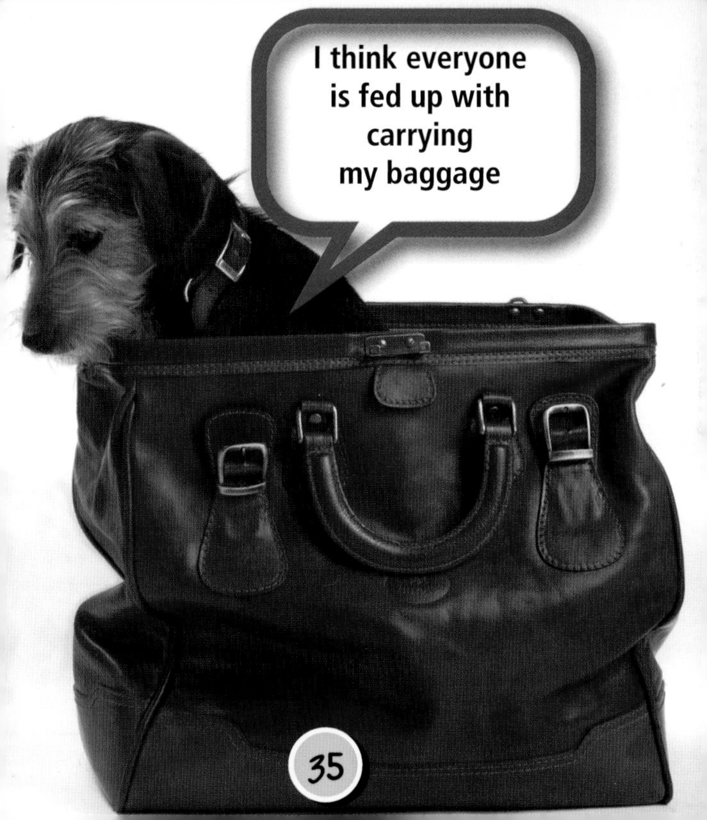

Of course I'm feeling deflated – everyone keeps letting me down

NAME: WOODY
AGE: 3
LIVES: MANHATTAN

I'm always trying to impress the buoys

NAME: EVA
AGE: 6
LIVES: SOUTH BEACH

I can't sustain my hard-man image

NAME: ROCKY
AGE: 7
LIVES: CHICAGO

38

I think I might be addicted to counselling

NAME: FRASIER
AGE: 5
LIVES: SEATTLE

I still haven't found what I'm looking for

NAME: BONIO
AGE: 6
LIVES: DUBLIN

41

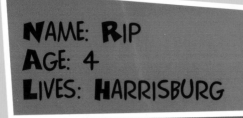

NAME: RIP
AGE: 4
LIVES: HARRISBURG

42

Things used to be much more black and white

NAME: JACOB
AGE: 5
LIVES: CHARLESTON

Do I look like I need a walk?

NAME: BARTY
AGE: 3
LIVES: MINNEAPOLIS

I have a chronic snow allergy

NAME: **R**UFUS
AGE: 9
LIVES: **B**OISE

NAME: BUSTER
AGE: 4
LIVES: DULUTH

I'm laughing inside

NAME: PETE
AGE: 7
LIVES: SANTA FE

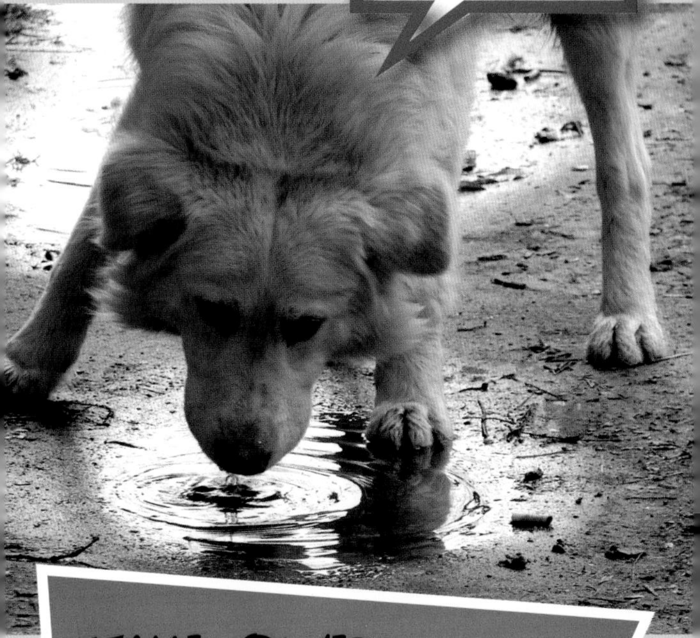

NAME: OLIVER
AGE: 6
LIVES: EL PASO

Everyone looks down on me

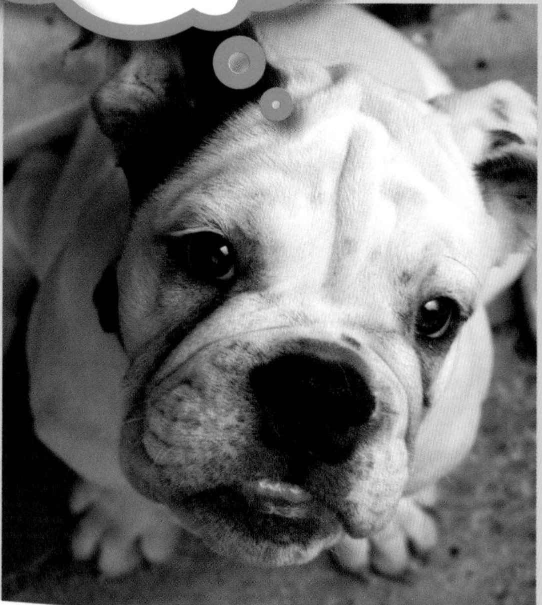

NAME: BART
AGE: 9
LIVES: DETROIT

I'm terrified of getting old and grey

NAME: SNOWY
AGE: 7
LIVES: CINCINNATI

51

I've gone right off solid food

NAME: JAWS
AGE: 3
LIVES: AMITY

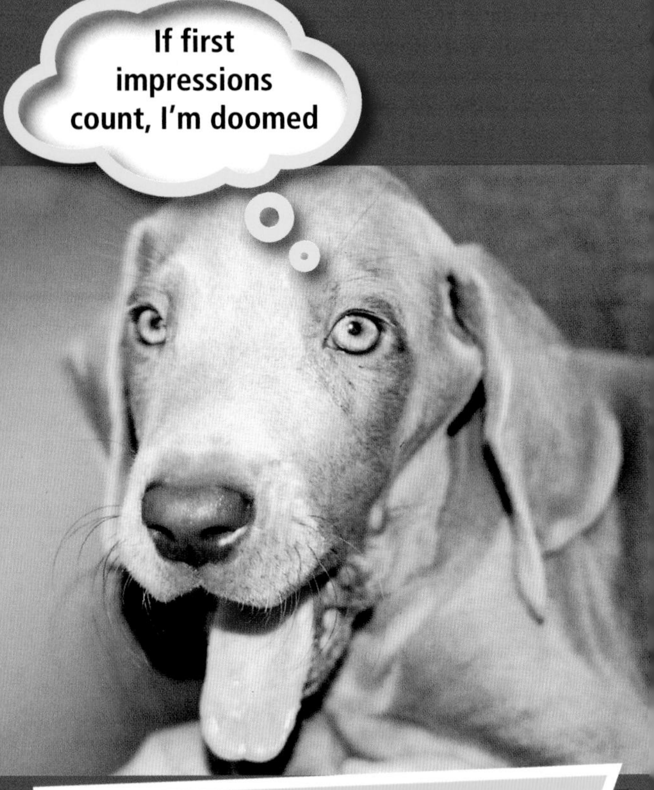

NAME: MITTY
AGE: 6
LIVES: RICHMOND

I'm a terrible back-seat driver

NAME: DAISY
AGE: 4
LIVES: LAFAYETTE

55

NAME: OZZY
AGE: 4
LIVES: BIRMINGHAM

56

I really need to stop eating joggers

NAME: ATTILA
AGE: 3
LIVES: SAN FRANCISCO

I wish people would stop giving me chocolate drops... what I really want is POWER!

NAME: KANE
AGE: 5
LIVES: LAS VEGAS

NAMES: ROMEO AND JULIET
AGES: 6 WEEKS AND 6 WEEKS
LIVE: BATON ROUGE

People don't take us seriously – they just call it 'puppy love'.

NAME: WILLARD
AGE: 3
LIVES: WASHINGTON

62

I think I've got things back-to-front

NAME: KAY
AGE: 7
LIVES: RENO

63

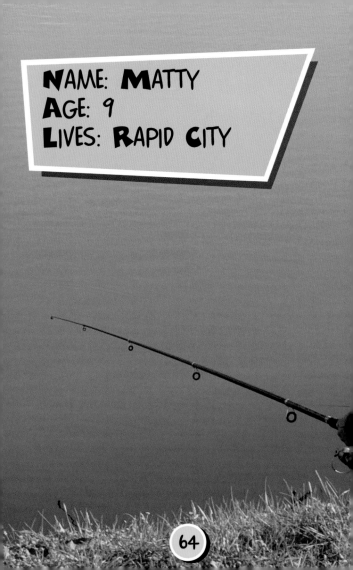

NAME: MATTY
AGE: 9
LIVES: RAPID CITY

64

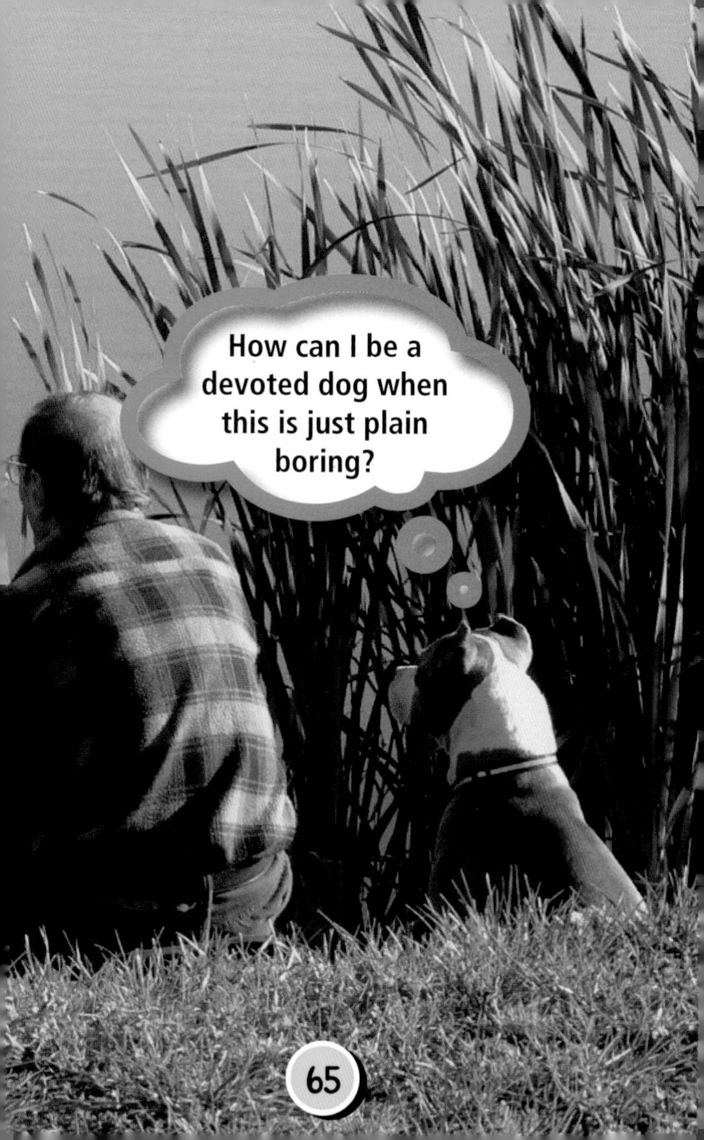
How can I be a devoted dog when this is just plain boring?

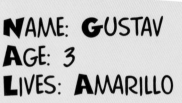

NAME: GUSTAV
AGE: 3
LIVES: AMARILLO

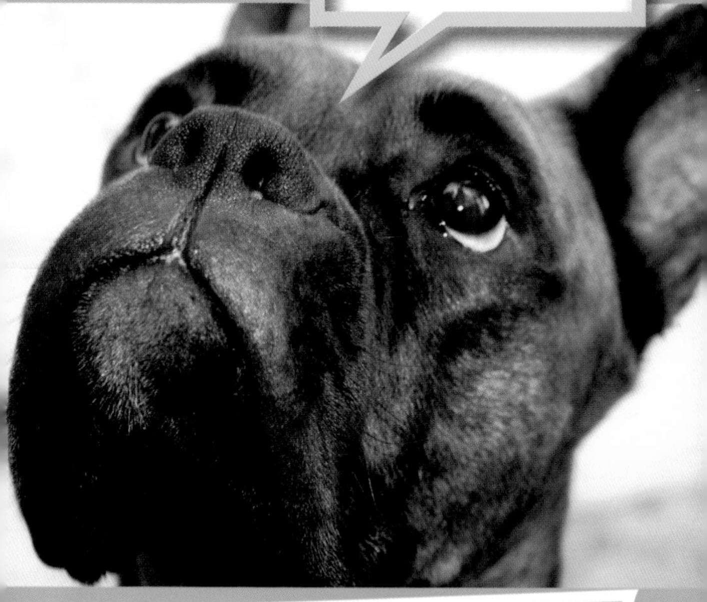

NAME: NELSON
AGE: 9
LIVES: OMAHA

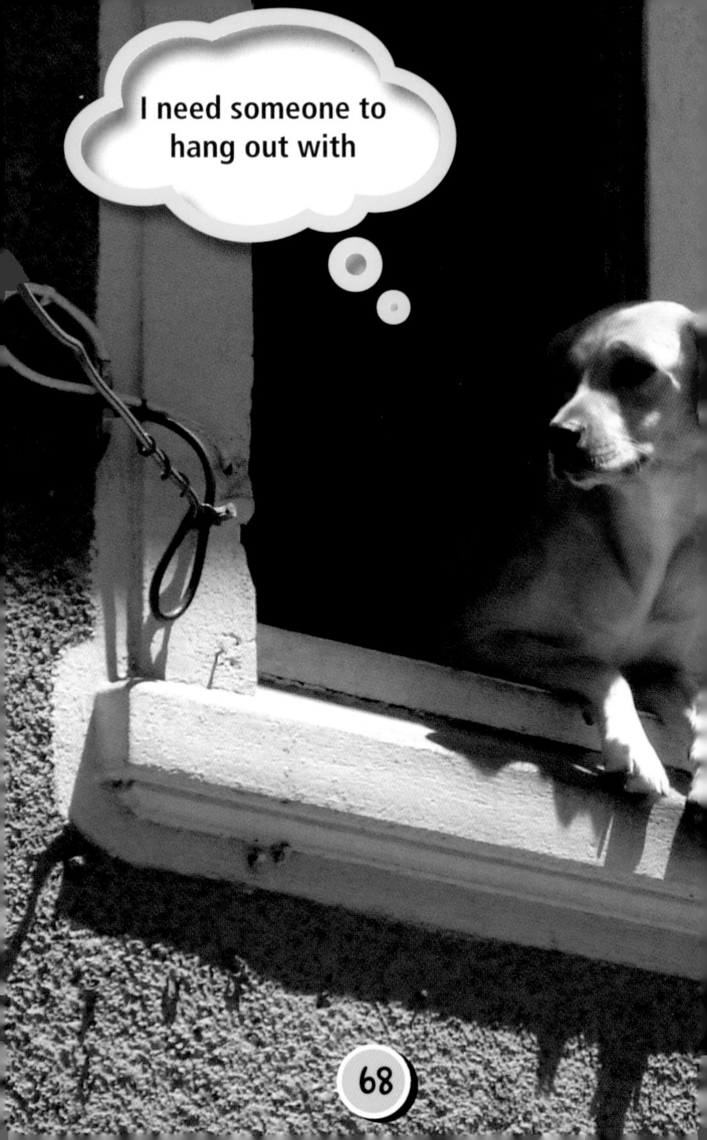
I need someone to hang out with

NAME: GOLDIE
AGE: 8
LIVES: CLEVELAND

NAME: GEORGE
AGE: 5
LIVES: DELAWARE

NAME: BILL
AGE: 4
LIVES: COLUMBUS

NAME: GIZZY
AGE: 5
LIVES: LUBBOCK

73

NAME: BASIL
AGE: 3
LIVES: DETROIT

74

NAME: HAL
AGE: 6
LIVES: NEWPORT

I feel fenced in

Name: McQueeny
Age: 3
Lives: New Orleans

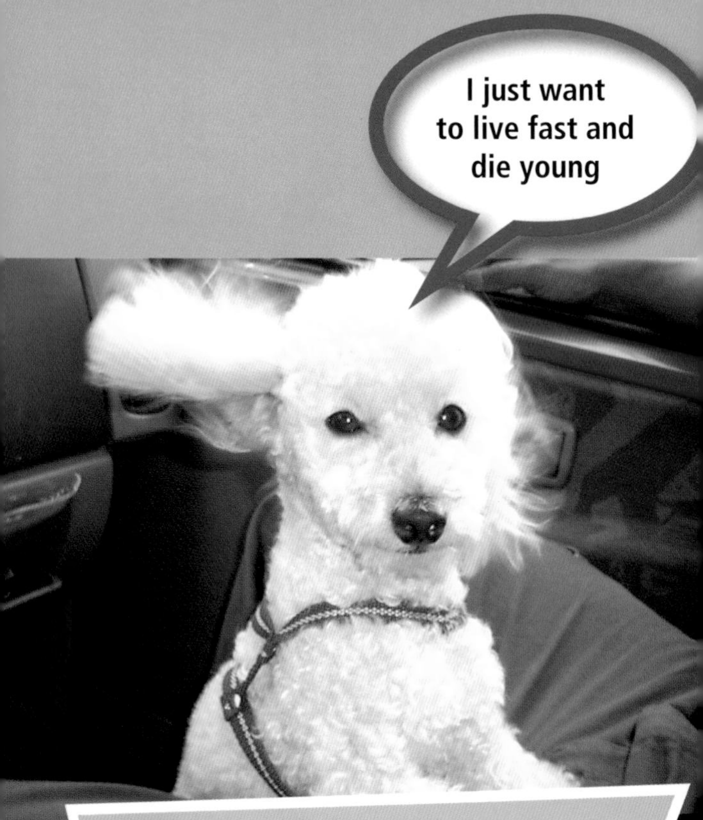

NAME: BABY
AGE: 4
LIVES: DAYTONA BEACH

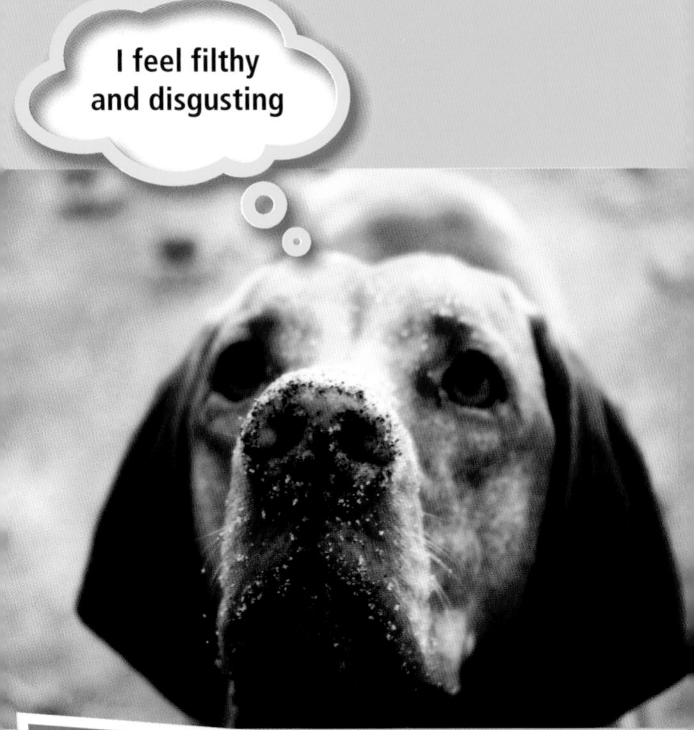

NAME: STINKY
AGE: 7
LIVES: DAYTON

I've got that
far-away feeling

NAME: LIVINGSTONE
AGE: 3
LIVES: BRIDGEPORT

NAME: HINDENBURG
AGE: 12
LIVES: GARY

82

I want to release the wolf inside... in the wild I'd have hunted people

NAME: DAISY
AGE: 3
LIVES: LINCOLN

I'm a goldfishophobic. If you don't keep dead still, they can sense your fear

NAME: ANGUS
AGE: 5
LIVES: BOISE

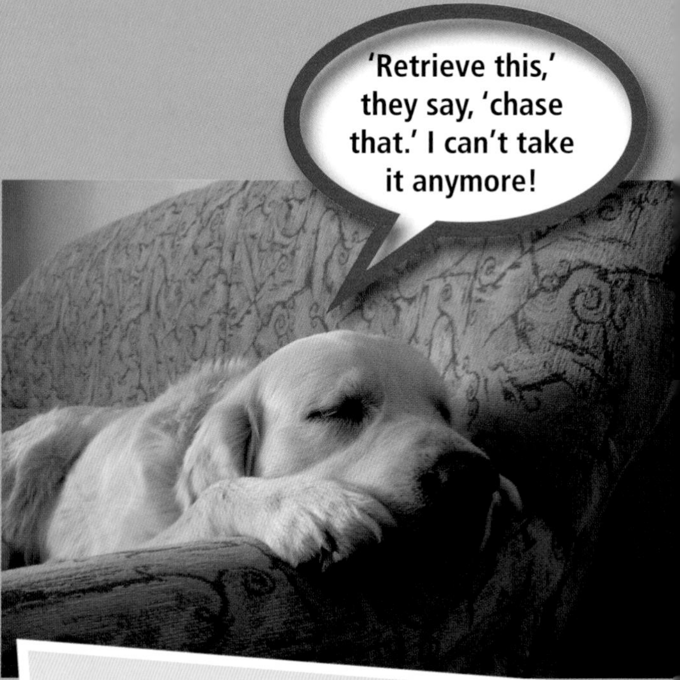

NAME: ROLY-POLY
AGE: 3
LIVES: BEVERLY HILLS

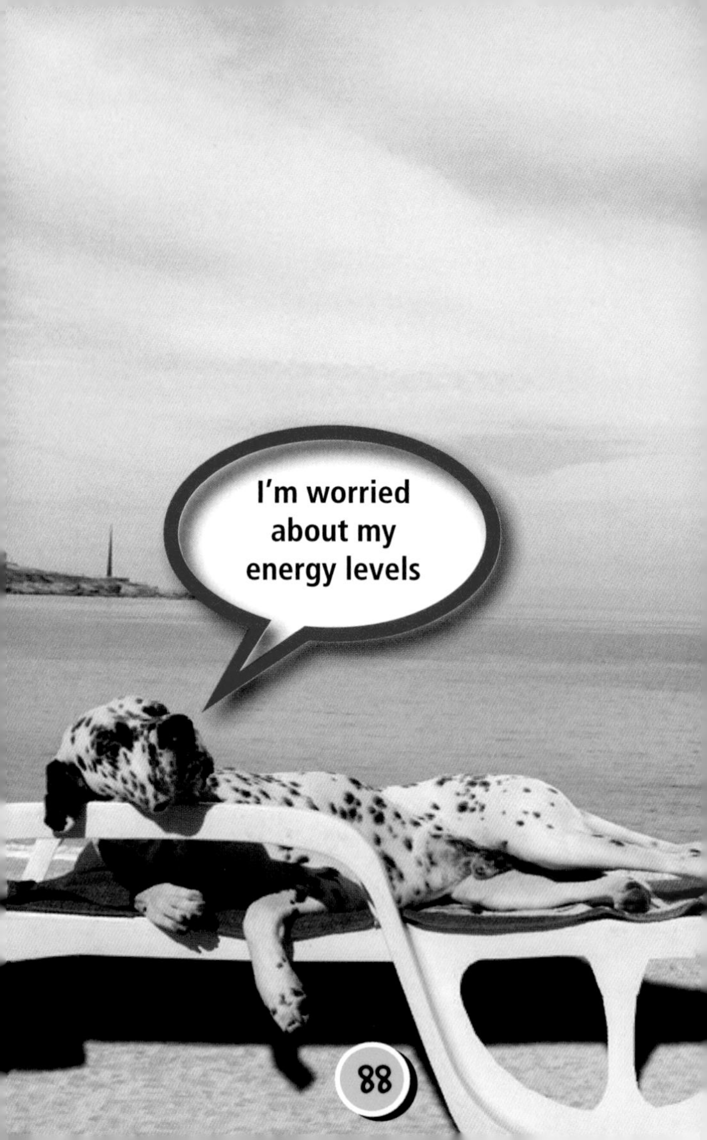
I'm worried about my energy levels

NAME: SPOTTY
AGE: 3
LIVES: SANTA BARBARA

NAME: CHUCK
AGE: 8
LIVES: WHITE SANDS

I left home because they called me 'Lassie'. Do I look like a film star?

NAME: LASSIE
AGE: 9
LIVES: NO FIXED ABODE

There's no looking back

NAME: JACK
AGE: 4
LIVES: NEW MEXICO

93

NAME: KEVIN
AGE: 3
LIVES: EL PASO

NAME: GUS
AGE: 5
LIVES: ALBUQUERQUE

95

NAME: FRANK
AGE: 9
LIVES: BILLINGS

NAME: KAISER
AGE: 5
LIVES: BOSTON

98

Wait until they find out I'm scared of squirrels

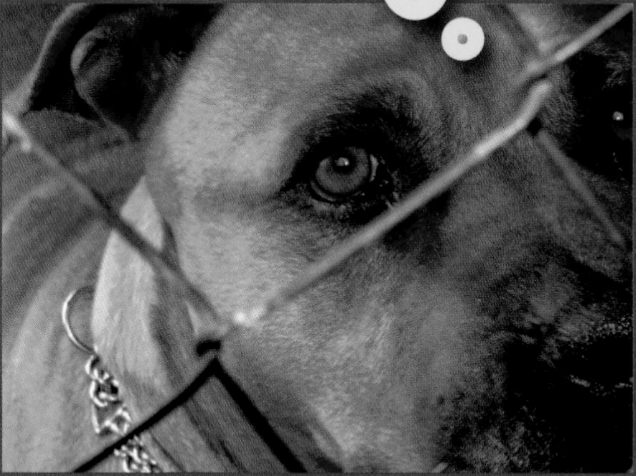

NAME: SAXON
AGE: 4
LIVES: AUSTIN

100

NAME: SAM
AGE: 3
LIVES: BOULDER

I'm not sure 'Grrrrrr' is working for me anymore

NAME: XERXES
AGE: 9
LIVES: SAN FRANCISCO

NAME: GNASHER
AGE: 10
LIVES: FORT WAYNE

104

I have a mailman addiction. Once I've had one, I just want another

I'm in need of support

NAME: JOSH
AGE: 4
LIVES: NEW JERSEY

NAME: CLEO
AGE: 1
LIVES: JACKSON

NAME: MITTY
AGE: 7
LIVES: DREAMWORLD

... and without a thought for his personal safety, Mitty the retriever jumped into the old dark water to retrieve the nuclear bomb, cunningly disguised by Dr Death to resemble a simple stick...

It's a beautiful day –
let's say 'to hell with
the analysis' and
go walkies

NAME: TRIGGER
AGE: 9
LIVES: NEW LONDON

NAME: RAMSEY
AGE: 4
LIVES: PALM SPRINGS

My whole life
is a blur

NAME: RAYMOND
AGE: 6
LIVES: NEW YORK

I'm on the lookout for Mr Right

NAME: LUCY
AGE: 9
LIVES: MAINE

I'd rather have been a poodle

NAME: TIDDLES
AGE: 4
LIVES: COS COB

115

I keep telling them I have a pollen allergy but what do I get? Walkies!

NAME: SNIFFY
AGE: 3
LIVES: DENVER

NAME: CASPER
AGE: 2
LIVES: LONG ISLAND

119

I'm tired of getting tied up at the office

NAME: BILL
AGE: 6
LIVES: NASHVILLE

We are all runts
in our family

NAME: VICKY
AGE: 3
LIVES: LEXINGTON

121

NAME: RODNEY
AGE: 7
LIVES: ST LOUIS

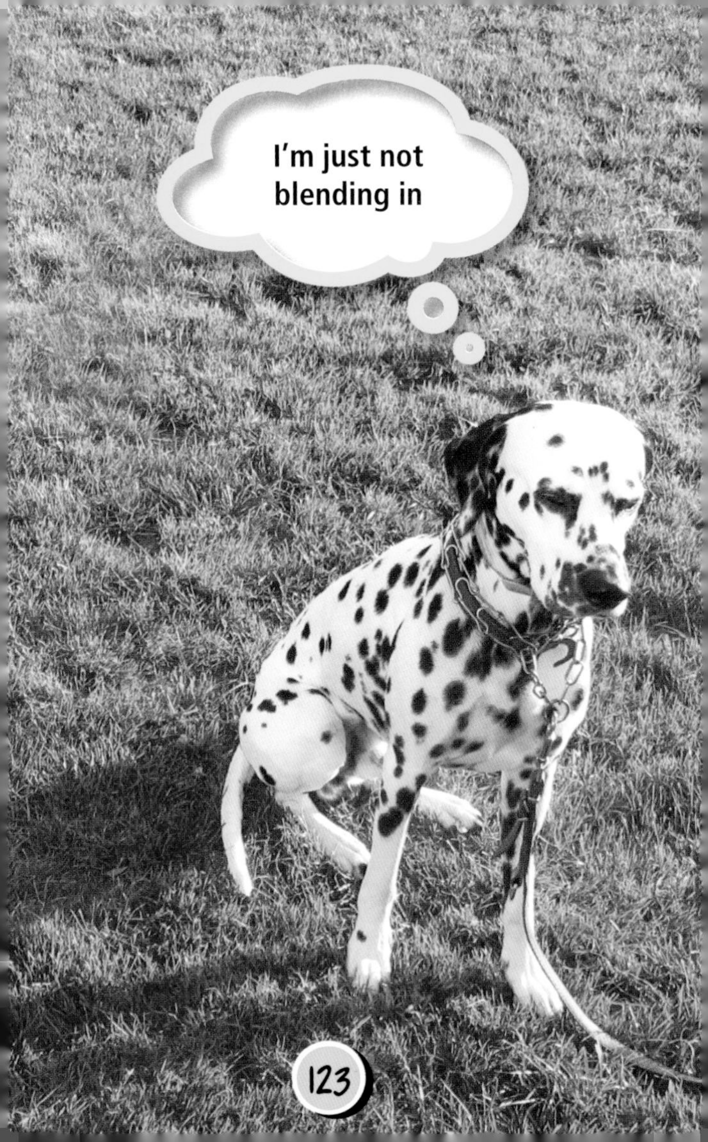
I'm just not blending in

NAME: PADDINGTON
AGE: 3
LIVES: LONDON

124

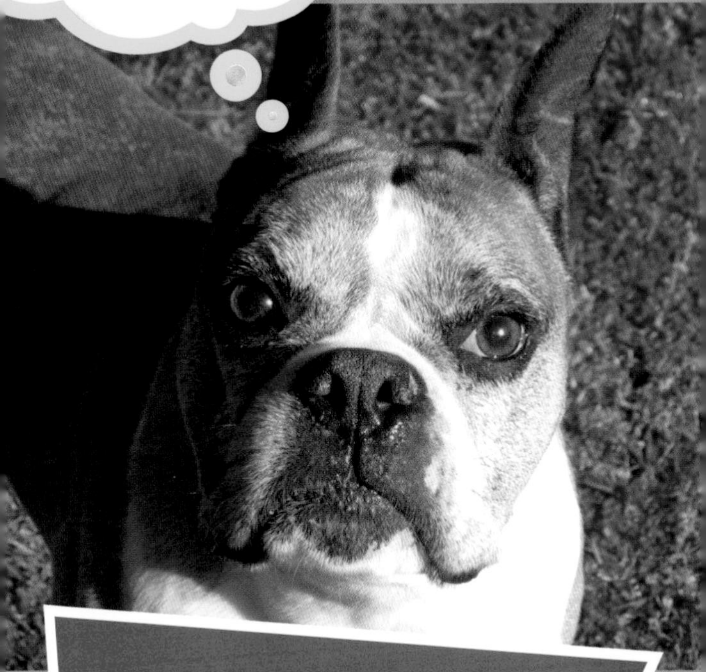

NAME: SPUTNIK
AGE: 4
LIVES: CAPE CANAVERAL

NAME: MARY
AGE: 8
LIVES: GREAT FALLS

I wish I could be a sheep and just follow the crowd

127

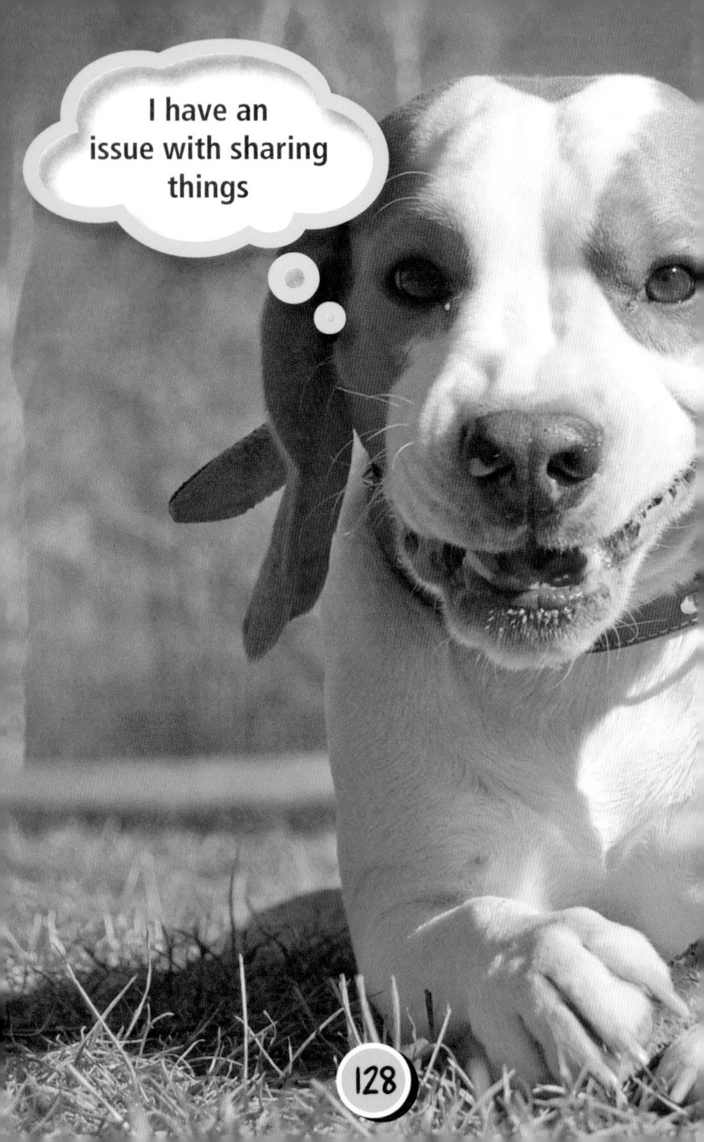
I have an issue with sharing things

NAME: CHRISTOPHER
AGE: 6
LIVES: MONTANA

NAME: MORRIS
AGE: 9
LIVES: BALTIMORE

130

I can't remember the last time someone said 'there's a good boy' to me

I find my overconfidence is getting me into a lot of trouble

NAME: CRAIG
AGE: 3
LIVES: CHICAGO

Cold nose, wagging tail, shiny coat... inside I'm a wreck

NAME: HOOPER
AGE: 5
LIVES: MILWAUKEE

133

NAME: JOE
AGE: 6
LIVES: SHREVEPORT

NAME: HULK
AGE: 8
LIVES: DENVER

NAME: JESSIE
AGE: 4
LIVES: KANSAS CITY

136

137

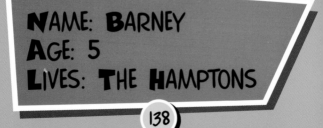

NAME: BARNEY
AGE: 5
LIVES: THE HAMPTONS

138

NAME: TIMMY
AGE: 9
LIVES: CHESAPEAKE

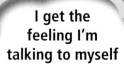

NAME: HUGH
AGE: 4
LIVES: MEMPHIS

141

NAME: GINSBERG
AGE: 9
LIVES: BERKELEY

I've gone from teenage depression to mid-life crisis in just two years

NAME: GILES
AGE: 3
LIVES: SANTA FE

The trouble is...
I'm the same size as
a rabbit
NAME: TOM
AGE: 5
LIVES: BEVERLY HILLS

I know I'm meant to chase mailmen, but I'm a modern dog – I prefer photographers

NAME: SAMSON
AGE: 4
LIVES: MIDLAND

NAME: BERTIE
AGE: 2
LIVES: BILLINGS

NAME: SALLY
AGE: 5
LIVES: WILMINGTON

149

NAMES: ASSORTED DOGS
AGES: VARIOUS
LIVE: OCEANSIDE

I've got a pack mentality

I've got a pack mentality

151

'Fetch,' 'Beg.'
It's not fair – what
I want to do
is write

NAME: REMUS
AGE: 7
LIVES: MONTGOMERY

NAME: **SPARTACUS**
AGE: 3
LIVES: **ATHENS**

NAME: NOGGIN
AGE: 1
LIVES: STOCKTON

I will never be happy until I eat live prey

NAME: LIONEL
AGE: 5
LIVES: PASADENA

159

Regrets?
I've had a few

NAME: FRANKIE
AGE: 9
LIVES: BROADWAY

I've no idea what I look like from the outside
NAME: SUZY
AGE: 5
LIVES: LAS VEGAS

NAME: RUSSELL
AGE: 4
LIVES: RENO

NAME: DROOPY
AGE: 3
LIVES: PENSACOLA

165

Trouble is... my bite really is worse than my bark

NAME: CHOMPER
AGE: 6
LIVES: VERMONT

I've become very jumpy

NAME: WOODY
AGE: 3
LIVES: HARRISBURG

169

I'm in love with a vet. It's so wrong... and yet it feels so right

NAME: FELICITY
AGE: 2
LIVES: DENVER

NAME: WIENER
AGE: 3
LIVES: BROOKLYN

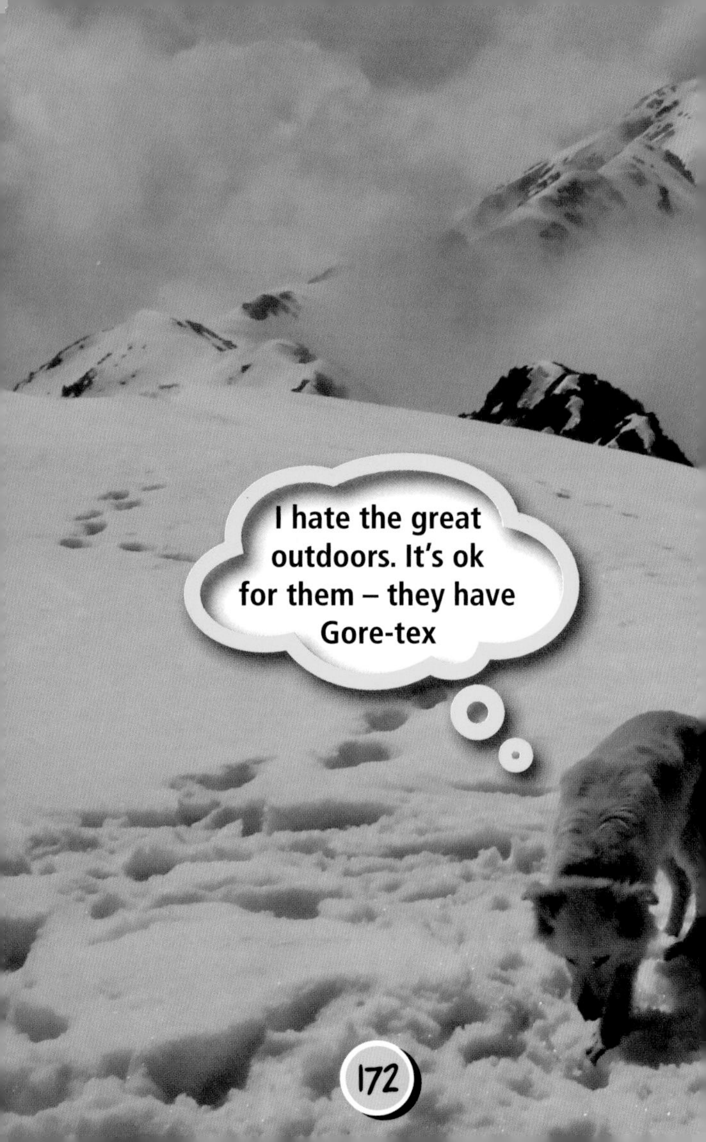
I hate the great outdoors. It's ok for them – they have Gore-tex

NAME: OTTO
AGE: 9
LIVES: ASPEN

173

NAME: WALTER
AGE: 10
LIVES: NEW YORK

PICTURE CREDITS